# Lizards

Annette Smith

## Contents

What Are Lizards? .......... 2
Where Lizards Live .......... 4
Shapes and Sizes .......... 6
Skin Colours .......... 8
Legs and Tails .......... 10
What Lizards Eat .......... 12
Geckos and Skinks .......... 14
Monitor Lizards .......... 18
Lizards Long Ago and Today .......... 22
Glossary .......... 24

# What Are Lizards?

Lizards are reptiles.
They cannot heat their own blood.

Lizards need to warm their bodies
in the hot sun during the day.

When their bodies are warm,
lizards are able to run and climb quickly,
as they hunt for food
or try to escape from predators.

# Where Lizards Live

Most lizards are found in tropical rainforests, or in the hot sands and rocky hills of deserts.

There are many places to find food and to hide from predators in rainforests and deserts.

Some lizards live in rainforests.

A lizard looks out for predators in a desert.

Some lizards can live in cooler places,
down near the sea or even high up in mountains.
But lizards are not found in the freezing ice
of Antarctica.

## Shapes and Sizes

Lizards are all shapes and sizes.
One of the smallest lizards is a tiny dwarf gecko.

The Komodo dragon is very big.
It is the largest lizard in the world.

a dwarf gecko

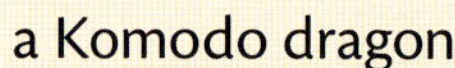

a Komodo dragon

Lizards have dry skin on their long bodies.
Their skin is covered with **scales**.
Lizards that live in burrows have flat scales,
to help them push through the soil.

A lizard's body is covered in scales.

## Skin Colours

Some lizards have very bright colours on their skin. Predators are often scared away when a lizard shows off its colours.

A chameleon can change the colour of its skin.

This green lizard is hard to spot on the green leaves.

Other lizards have green or grey–brown skin.
If they stay very still,
predators do not see them
hiding among the branches of trees.

Many lizards have spots or stripes on their skin.
It is hard to see these lizards in dry grass.

## Legs and Tails

Most lizards have short legs, with five toes on each foot. The toes have soft pads or sharp claws for climbing or attacking **prey**.

a legless lizard

Some lizards do not have legs at all.
They are called legless lizards.
These lizards have long bodies
and look like snakes.

Many lizards have long tails.
Some have short, fat tails.

# What Lizards Eat

Most lizards eat insects.

They catch ants, termites, beetles, butterflies and moths.

Some lizards eat spiders, worms, snails
and other small lizards, too.
Lizards that eat snails have flat, round teeth,
for crushing the shells.

Many large lizards eat plants and fruit.
Some even eat seaweed.

# Geckos and Skinks

Geckos and skinks are small lizards.

Geckos hunt for food at night.
They have large eyes to help them see in the dark.
Geckos do not have **eyelids**.
They clean the dust and dirt from their eyes
with their long tongues.

Geckos can climb up the sides of wet rocks. They have lots of tiny hairs under their toes, to help their feet stick to the rock.

Most skinks have shiny, brown scales, small eyes and long tails.

Many skinks live on the ground, and hide in the cracks of rocks and logs. Lots of skinks are found in gardens and parks.

If a predator catches a skink or a gecko by the tail, it can escape. The lizard's tail breaks off.

This skink has had its tail broken off.

## Monitor Lizards

Monitor lizards are very large lizards. They like to live in sandy places where they can dig burrows.

Monitor lizards often stand up straight
on their huge hind legs to look for prey,
or to check for predators that could be nearby.

If predators come too close,
the monitor lizards swing their enormous tails
to frighten them away.

Monitors have long, **forked** tongues, like a snake's tongue.
They flick their tongues in and out quickly, to smell the ground and taste the air.

Their teeth are very sharp.
Sometimes, they feed on dead animals.
The Komodo dragon is a monitor lizard.
It will often hunt wild pigs, deer and monkeys.

## Lizards Long Ago and Today

Lizards have been living on Earth for millions of years.

They have many clever ways of staying safe from predators, and hunting for food.

Lizards are an important part of our **wildlife**, today.

a frilled lizard

# Glossary

**eyelids** *(noun)* folds of skin to cover the eyes

**forked** *(adjective)* shaped like the end of a fork

**prey** *(noun)* an animal that is being hunted

**scales** *(noun)* small, thin plates on an animal's body

**wildlife** *(noun)* animals that live in their own habitat